NOW YOU SEE IT!

SMALL TO SCARY ANIMALS

By Aubre Andrus

SCHOLASTIC INC.

Photo Credits
Photos ©: cover top main: Daniel J Cox/Getty Images; cover top inset: Cordier Sylvain/hemis.fr/Getty Images; cover bottom main: PHOTO 24/Getty Images; cover bottom inset: Wim van den Heever/Tetra Images/Corbis Images; back cover top: Donyanedomam/Thinkstock; back cover bottom: Daniel J Cox/Getty Images; 1 top: Suzi Eszterhas/Ardea; 1 bottom: Cafebeanz Company/Dreamstime; 3 paper texture and throughout: CG Textures; 3 main: Kitchner Bain/Dreamstime; 4 and textured backgrounds throughout: CG Textures; 5: Daniel J Cox/Getty Images; 7: PHOTO 24/Getty Images; 9: Isselee/Dreamstime.com; 11: David Cayless/Getty Images; 13: Donyanedomam/Thinkstock; 15: Bennett, Darren/Animals Animals; 17: Gerry Ellis/Minden Pictures/National Geographic Creative; 19: Aaron Amat/Shutterstock, Inc.; 21: tantrik71/Shutterstock, Inc.; 23: NewSaetiew/iStockphoto; 25: Suzi Eszterhas/Ardea; 27: Cafebeanz Company/Dreamstime; 29: Mylaphotography/Dreamstime; 31: Georgette Douwma/Minden Pictures; 33: James Hager/Media Bakery; 35: Anthony Bannister/Getty Images; 37: Raimund Linke/Media Bakery; 39: genesisgraphics/iStockphoto; 41: Wolfgang Kaehler/LightRocket/Getty Images; 43: Paul Nicklen/National Geographic Creative; 45: Jupiterimages/Thinkstock; 47: Shchipkova Elena/Dreamstime; 49: Mark Moffett/Minden Pictures; 51: kikkerdirk/Thinkstock; 53: Karin Van Ijzendoorn/Dreamstime; 55: TwilightShow/Thinkstock; 57: Heiko Kiera/Shutterstock, Inc.; 59: Mgkuijpers/Dreamstime; 61: M&G Therin-Weise/Media Bakery; 63: wrangel/Thinkstock; 64 top: Donyanedomam/Thinkstock; 64 bottom: Daniel J Cox/Getty Images.

Copyright © 2016 by Scholastic Inc.

Library of Congress Cataloging-in-Publication Data available.

ISBN 978-0-545-88960-5

10 9 8 7 6 5 4 3 2 1   16 17 18 19 20 21

Printed in Malaysia   106
First printing, January 2016

Designed by Marissa Asuncion

Don't you just love baby animals? From cubs to pups to calves, you can't help but smile when you see one. But they don't stay small for very long. Many animals change from cute babies to big, scary adults in a few years—or even just a few months!

GRAY WOLF

Newborn wolf pups weigh only one pound. When they turn three weeks old, they leave their dens to play outside and learn to howl. But when they're this young, their howls sound more like squeaks!

GRAY WOLF

Wolves have 42 teeth. That's 10 more than an adult human! With sharp teeth and strong jaws, wolves can easily hunt large animals like deer and moose.

SCARY · SCARY · SCARY · SCARY · SCARY
SCARY · SCARY · SCARY · SCARY · SCARY
SCARY · SCARY · SCARY · SCARY · SCARY

AFRICAN ELEPHANT

A baby elephant, or calf, is cute but often clumsy. It spends all day learning how to control its long trunk, floppy ears, and thick legs. Even with practice, baby elephants still trip and fall sometimes!

AFRICAN ELEPHANT

An elephant's trunk is more than just a long nose–it can grab things, too. But you don't want to get in an elephant's way. Its trunk is so strong that it can knock over a tree!

GRIZZLY BEAR

Bear cubs are born during the winter when bears hibernate, or sleep, in a den for months at a time. Bears can nap for as long as seven months, but they have to wake up once the new babies arrive!

SCARY • SCARY • SCARY • SCARY • SCARY • SC
ARY • SCARY • SCARY • SCARY • SCA
RY • SCARY • SCARY • SCAR
ARY • SCARY • SCAR
RY • SC
ARY

GRIZZLY BEAR

Hikers never want to meet a bear on their path, especially a bear that is eating or with its cubs. That's why they carry bear spray, which hurts the bear's eyes and nose so it becomes confused and can't attack anyone.

CHIMPANZEE

A chimpanzee is the animal that is most like a human. Chimps even kiss and hug like we do! Baby chimpanzees like to be carried and often ride on their mothers' backs.

CHIMPANZEE

Chimpanzees are like humans, but they're much stronger. They may be as much as seven times stronger than us! When male chimps get angry, they scream, stomp their feet, and throw rocks to show that they're upset.

HIPPOPOTAMUS

Some baby hippos are born in the water and they'll spend most of their days there. They can even eat underwater! Luckily, their moms protect them from being taken by hungry predators like crocodiles.

HIPPOPOTAMUS

Hippopotamuses are one of the most dangerous animals in Africa. They have extra-large mouths, huge tusks, and sharp teeth. They can weigh up to 8,000 pounds. That's twice as much as a car!

LION

Lion cubs stay close to their families, which are called "prides." Cubs like to play with their mothers' tails. They also enjoy cuddling with their brothers and sisters.

LION

The powerful lion is known as "the king of the jungle." Its roar is so loud that it can be heard up to five miles away. If any animal makes a lion angry, they'll hear about it!

small · small · small · small · small · small · small · s
small · small · small · small · small · small · small
small · small · small · small · small
small · small · small · s
small

STINGRAY

Baby stingrays are called "pups." Their eyes are located on top of their bodies, but their mouths and noses are found on their underbellies. This makes them look like they're smiling!

small · small · small · small · small · s
small · small · small · small · small · small · sr
small · small · small · small · small · small · small · s
small · small · small · small · small · small · small · sr
small · small · small · small · small · small · small · si

STINGRAY

Stingrays like to bury themselves in the sands of shallow water, so make sure you don't step on one—they really do sting! Their "tail" is filled with dangerous venom, which can be very painful. Ouch!

PORCUPINE

Baby porcupines, called "porcupettes," are born with soft quills that soon turn hard and spiky. Some types of porcupines are good at climbing trees because of their curved claws and strong tails.

small · small

32

PORCUPINE

Never pet a porcupine! They have more than 30,000 quills on their bodies that may look soft but can be as sharp as needles. Their quills stand up when they feel threatened, which makes them look bigger and helps keep predators away.

MOOSE

Baby moose, or calves, are born with long, skinny legs. They're actually very athletic, and they can run and swim at a young age. Moose mothers stay nearby as the calves grow up to protect them from wolves and bears.

MOOSE

Picking a fight with a moose is definitely a *moose*-take. Their antlers are as dangerous as they look, but so are their hooves, which are large and sharp. Moose can kick really hard, so watch out!

small · small · small · small · small · small · small · sm
small · small · small · small · small · small · sma
small · small · small · small · small · small · sma
small · small · small · small · small · sma
small · small · sm
small · small
sma

LEOPARD SEAL

Leopard seal babies, called "pups," have spotted fur–that's how they got their name! When they're young, leopard seal pups eat krill, which are small shrimp-like creatures that live in the water.

small · small · small · small · small · small · small
small · small · small · small · small · small · small ·
small · small · small · small · small · small · small
small · small · small · small · small · small · small ·

LEOPARD SEAL

Leopard seals can swim really fast. When they're hungry, they quickly leap out of the water and splash onto the edge of the ice to catch birds, penguins, or other seals. Sneaky!

LYNX

A baby lynx could pass for a cuddly pet kitten, except for its tail, which is short and stubby! A lynx's fur is also extra thick to keep it warm during the winter.

LYNX

Lynx are excellent hunters. The funny tufts of hair on their ears actually help them to hear well. They also have sharp eyes that can see a mouse from 250 feet away. That's almost the length of a football field!

POISON DART FROG

Once frog tadpoles hatch from their eggs, they swim onto their dad's back. The father frog carries the tadpoles to a safe spot in the pond so they can grow. In just three months' time, they'll be frogs!

POISON DART FROG

Don't try to pick up a poison dart frog in the wild. Its colorful skin may look pretty, but it's actually poisonous and contains deadly venom. These dangerous frogs have very few predators and eat spiders and insects like ants and termites.

HYENA

A baby hyena looks like a dog, but it's actually more similar to a cat. Hyenas live in clans, or families, of up to 100. Sometimes they even fight with their brothers and sisters!

HYENA

Hyenas like to "laugh," but they're not jokesters. They work together to hunt large animals like wildebeests and zebras. They like to eat every last bit of their meals—even the bones!

SCARY
SCARY
SCARY
CARY
SCARY

SCARY • SCARY • SCARY • SCARY
SCARY • SCARY • SCARY • SCARY • SCAR

SNAKE

Which came first: the snake or the egg? Most snakes hatch from eggs, just like chickens do. The mother snake keeps the eggs warm before they hatch, and she can lay more than 50 eggs at a time.

SNAKE

Snakes can strike in the blink of an eye. Despite their skinny size, they can eat some large animals, like rodents and birds. They just swallow them whole! One meal can make a snake feel full for months. Imagine that!

RHINOCEROS

Rhinoceros babies, called "calves," like to play. They practice charging and fighting with other young rhinos. But don't worry—it's just for fun! Their horns haven't grown yet, so they can't cause any real damage.

RHINOCEROS

Rhinos are thought to have bad tempers. In reality, they can't see very well, so they get scared easily. They'll charge at almost anything—even a rock or a tree!

Even the smallest animal babies can grow up to become powerful, scary creatures. So don't call those furry youngsters "cute"– soon, they may be more fierce than friendly!